W9-AKD-989

DATE DUE

JE 16 '89 DEC 1 0 94		
JY 5 '89 MR 1 4 95		
DE 26 '89 AUG 1 1 97		
FE 27 '90 FE 16 01		
MR 23 '90 JY 16 02		
JE 28 '90		
JY 16 '91		
JY 30 '91		
JA 23 '92		
JY 23 '92		
NOV 29 '93		
NOV 3 '00		

$10.95

598.9   Green, Carl R
GRE   The peregrine falcon

THE PEREGRINE FALCON

BY
CARL R. GREEN
WILLIAM R. SANFORD

EDITED BY
DR. HOWARD SCHROEDER

Professor in Reading and Language Arts
Dept. of Elementary Education
Mankato State University

PRODUCED AND DESIGNED BY
BAKER STREET PRODUCTIONS
Mankato, MN

CRESTWOOD HOUSE
Mankato, Minnesota

LIBRARY OF CONGRESS CATALOGING IN PUBLICATION DATA

Sanford, William R. (William Reynolds)
 The peregrine falcon.

 (Wildlife, habits & habitat)
 SUMMARY: Describes the physical characteristics, habitat, behavior, and life cycle of this small bird of prey and briefly examines the sport of falconry.
 1. Peregrine falcon--Juvenile literature. (1. Peregrine falcon. 2. Falcons) I. Green, Carl R. II. Title. III. Series.
 QL696.F34S26   1986   598'.918   86-2670
 ISBN 0-89686-271-2 (lib. bdg.)

International Standard Book Number:	Library of Congress Catalog Card Number:
Library Binding 0-89686-271-2	86-2670

ILLUSTRATION CREDITS:

Annie Griffiths/DRK Photo: Cover
Phil & Loretta Hermann: 4, 7, 20, 36
Warren Garst/Tom Stack & Assoc.: 8
Brian Parker/Tom Stack & Assoc.: 12, 14, 29, 35
Bob Williams: 17, 32-33
Steve Kraseman/DRK Photo: 18, 23, 30, 40, 42-43
W. Perry Conway/Tom Stack & Assoc.: 24-25
Jeff Foott/DRK Photo: 39

CRESTWOOD HOUSE

Hwy. 66 South, Box 3427
Mankato, MN 56002-3427

TABLE OF CONTENTS

A peregrine falcon roosts with a hood on its head.

INTRODUCTION:

A peregrine's first hunt

The cold Colorado air cut through Marcie's parka. Her nose felt numb. She shivered and waited for the sun to rise.

Beside her, a peregrine falcon named Prince perched on his roost. A hood covered the bird's head and kept him quiet. Marcie was worried about the young falcon. This would be his first free flight. She had helped her uncle raise him. Now, what if he flew away and didn't come back?

Marcie looked at her uncle. Fred Tucker was a naturalist who had spent most of his life studying birds. At the moment, he was standing on the edge of the mesa. Below them, the plains lay quiet and dark. The nearest town was far away. Prince jumped and flapped his wings. Leather strings held him to the roost. He seemed to sense Marcie's excitement.

"Look! The sun is coming up," Marcie said. "I guess it's time for Prince to fly."

Dr. Tucker walked over to the falcon. "Okay, Prince, this is your big chance," he said. "You're good at catching the pigeons we throw to you in the barn. Now let's see if you can hunt real game."

5

Marcie put on a long leather glove. Prince stepped onto the leather sleeve. Marcie could feel his sharp talons grip her arm. She took off the falcon's hood and strings. The falcon's large black eyes blinked in the morning light.

Dr. Tucker nodded his okay, and Marcie moved her arm upward. The peregrine soared into the air. "Go, Prince, go!" she called.

The young falcon flew upward. Each powerful beat of his wings sent him higher. In a minute he was a small black dot against the blue sky.

Marcie tried to see the prairie as Prince would. But his eyes were so much better than hers! She looked for birds, knowing that peregrines like to kill their prey in the air. Nothing moved. High above them, Prince glided in a large circle.

Then it happened. A prairie hen flew up from its hiding place. From a thousand feet (300 m) up, Prince spotted the fast-moving bird. He folded his wings back and dived. The falcon dropped out of the sky at over a hundred miles an hour (160 kph).

Prince's aim was perfect. His curved talons struck the hen and killed it. At the same instant, the peregrine spread his wings to break his fall. He turned back toward his roost with the dead hen held tightly in his talons.

"He did it!" Marcie yelled. "And he's coming back!"

Dr. Tucker put an arm around his niece. "You've done a good job of raising him," he said. "Once he can feed himself, we'll release him. It's up to Prince and his brothers and sisters to bring peregrines back to this area."

Marcie hugged her uncle. "He's so beautiful! It makes me cry when I think that peregrines almost became extinct."

The peregrine falcon nearly became extinct in the 1960's.

CHAPTER ONE:

Peregrine falcons belong to an order of birds called the Falconiformes. The group includes vultures, kites, hawks, eagles, and falcons. Except for vultures, all of these birds hunt and kill other animals for their food. With their hooked beaks and strong talons, the Falconiformes are excellent predators. All of the Falconiformes are daytime hunters.

The peregrine falcon does its hunting during the day.

A large family

The peregrine falcon is the best known of the fifty-eight birds in the falcon family. *Peregrine* comes from a word that means, "one who wanders." This "wandering" falcon has earned its name. Some of Canada's tundra peregrines, for example, fly to Brazil each winter.

Peregrine falcons are found in every part of the world except Antarctica. Kings once trained them to hunt and bring back kills. This sport, called falconry, is still popular. In the 1960's, however, the American falcon came close to extinction. Most of the damage was done by poisons that farmers used to kill insects. The worst poison was DDT. By the time naturalists learned of DDT's effect on wildlife, it was almost too late.

North America's peregrines divide into three subspecies. Each subspecies lives in its own territory. Only experts can tell the three peregrines apart.

The American peregrine is known by the scientific name of *Falco peregrinus anatum*. At one time, people called this falcon a duck hawk. That was a poor name, for falcons aren't hawks and they seldom kill ducks. The American peregrine was once found across the eastern United States and southern Canada. In the west, the species was found from California to Mexico. DDT poisoning hit this subspecies the hardest. Today, naturalists are working hard to save the American peregrine from extinction.

The smaller tundra peregrine *(Falco peregrinus tundrius)* lives farther north. Tundra peregrines range across the treeless regions of Alaska and Canada. They are also found in Greenland. Peale's peregrine *(Falco peregrinus pealei)* is the third North American subspecies. This western bird ranges from Oregon northward to Alaska and the Aleutian Islands. Peale's peregrine is the largest of the three subspecies. The tundra and Peale's peregrines have escaped the worst effects of DDT poisoning.

Most peregrines are slate blue on the back and wings. The top of the head is black. Black feathers around the eyes reduce glare and improve the bird's vision. The white underside of a peregrine's wings, tail, and chest show more bands of dark feathers. Bird lovers agree with ancient kings: Peregrines are one of nature's most beautiful birds.

A bird sized for speed and killing

A peregrine falcon is a medium-sized bird about the size of a crow. Female peregrines are larger and heavier than the males. An average female (called a falcon) weighs a little over two pounds (1 kg). The female is eighteen inches (46 cm) in length from beak to square tail. Her long, pointed wings measure forty-five inches (114 cm) from tip to tip. The male bird (called a tiercel) is only two-thirds the size of his mate. Thus, a typical tiercel weighs only one and one-half pounds (.7 kg). His body is two inches (5 cm) shorter and his wings are four inches (10 cm) shorter than the female.

A peregrine's feathers make its high-speed flight possible. The feathers lie close to its streamlined body. Like all birds, peregrines lose their feathers and grow new ones. This process is called molting. A peregrine's molt lasts from April to October. It loses only a few feathers at a time. If too many feathers fell out, peregrines wouldn't be able to fly.

In flight, a peregrine's wings look long and pointed. Close to the body, however, the wing is wide and strong. This gives the falcon the lift it needs to carry a heavy kill. In level flight, these swift falcons reach speeds of sixty miles per hour (96 kph). During a dive (called a stoop by falconers) peregrines reach their highest speeds. They fold their wings halfway back and drop like a missile. An air force pilot once clocked a diving peregrine at 175 mph (280 kph)!

The peregrine's feet and beak are also designed for killing. Each yellow foot has four toes, three in front and one behind. Each toe ends in a curved claw called a talon. When a peregrine dives at its prey, it strikes first with the razor-sharp back talons. This blow usually kills the prey instantly. If the prey is still alive, the peregrine uses its strong, tan-colored beak. One slashing bite with that hooked beak will break the back of smaller birds.

A bird that sees everything

The peregrine's large eyes give it superior vision. Each black, shiny eye weighs about one ounce (28 g). If a falcon were as big as you are, its eyes would weigh four pounds (1.8 kg) each! A falcon's eyes are set toward the front of its head. It cannot see in all directions at one time. Look at what happens when it hears a noise from behind. The bird will turn its head all the way to the rear! The peregrine doesn't see colors as well as you do. But its ability to see at a distance is eight times better than yours.

Let's follow a flying peregrine. The peregrine looks down at the land with sudden turns of its head. When it sees movement, it brings its sharpest vision to bear

The peregrine falcon can kill its prey either in the air or on the ground.

on that spot. This action works like the zoom lens of a camera. Everything in that small area jumps into sharp focus. If it sees a pigeon, the hungry peregrine will begin its dive. A stooping peregrine can track and hit a dodging pigeon from a thousand feet up!

Naturalists do not know how peregrines find their way back to their nests. They guess that the bird somehow remembers the look of nearby fields, woods, and rivers. Peregrines are equally at home in big cities. To them, a tall building is just another natural stone cliff. City peregrines nest on building ledges and hunt pigeons and starlings.

The peregrine's other senses

Along with keen eyesight, peregrines have good hearing. Peregrines don't make warning cries, but they listen to the warning calls of other birds. A peregrine is usually silent while it's hunting. Around its own nest (called an eyrie), a peregrine makes a number of calls. To attract a mate, the tiercel makes a series of tweeting and wailing cries. If a human comes too close to the eyrie, the peregrine issues an angry warning cry: *"cack, cack, cack."* The falcon will fly directly at the face of the stranger if the warning doesn't work.

Taste and smell are less important. Peregrines don't have many taste buds on their tongues. Thus, a peregrine will eat birds that taste terrible to humans. Similarly, peregrines can smell odors, but they don't use this sense in hunting. When its dinner is flying far below, the peregrine must depend on its eyes.

A long-lived bird — if it's lucky

Left alone, peregrines may live as long as twenty years. One famous falcon nested on the Sun Life building in Montreal, Canada for eighteen years. Many peregrines die in their first year of life, however. Even without DDT, the peregrine's habitat holds many dangers.

Today, the American peregrine has almost vanished. The tundra and Peale's peregrines have been less affected by the poisons. They can still be found in many of their northern and western ranges.

If they can avoid danger, a peregrine can live to be twenty years old.

CHAPTER TWO:

Peregrine falcons were once found over most of North America. Their favorite habitat is a rocky cliff that overlooks open country. These cliffs are often found near rivers and lakes and along the seacoast. A peregrine habitat also needs a food supply of songbirds, pigeons, and waterfowl.

A yearly migration

Peregrines spend their summers in the northern half of their range. When winter drives the smaller birds south, the peregrines join the migration. Cold weather doesn't seem to bother them, but they must have food. Tundra peregrines fly the farthest of all falcons. Some fly to Florida and Central America. Others travel all the way to Brazil. American peregrines and Peale's peregrines do not fly as far. The young birds don't need a guide. Instinct tells them where to go when the food supply flies south.

A territorial bird

Even before the DDT disaster, there weren't many American peregrines. Naturalists believe that the U.S. never had more than a thousand mated pairs. The numbers are small because each tiercel marks out its own territory. The territory may be large or small, depending on the supply of game. A tiercel will drive away other male peregrines that enter his territory.

Once a tiercel finds a mate, the pair chooses a site for their eyrie. The peregrines do not build nests in trees. Instead, they scrape out a hollow on the ground for their eggs. Peregrines prefer a cliff ledge (or a building ledge). But they will also nest in hollow trees or in old eagles' nests. Peregrines return to their eyries year after year. Some eyries have been in use for over a century.

A predator's diet

Imagine that you're walking out in the country. All around you, larks are singing their pretty songs. Suddenly, a dark shape drops out of the sky. One of the larks twists and dodges, but it's no use. The peregrine falcon hits the lark in a burst of feathers. You can see the hunter flying off with its prey. For just a moment, you feel angry. Why should predators be allowed to kill harmless songbirds?

Naturalists tell us that predators play an important role in nature. Without predators, the larks and other small birds would breed too fast. Soon there wouldn't be enough food and they would starve. Many times, the predators catch the weaker and older birds. That means that only the strongest larks survive to raise their chicks. Besides, every species eats something else. Do we get upset because pelicans catch fish? Or because herons feed on frogs?

Peregrine falcons prefer to catch their prey on the wing. A typical peregrine will kill and eat pigeons, small gulls and ducks. It will also kill quail, pheasants, larks, bluejays, orioles, and dozens of other birds. The females

Robins

Pheasant

Gull

The peregrine kills a variety of birds for food.

hunt larger birds that the smaller tiercels cannot bring down. If peregrines are hungry enough, they will eat fish, insects, and dead animals.

After making a kill, the peregrine finds a safe eating spot. It usually flies to a nearby tree, or to a cliff ledge. If the prey is heavy, the peregrine eats it on the ground. It first plucks the feathers from the dead bird. Then it strips off the meat. Only the head, wings, tail, and bones are left behind. Females with newly hatched chicks (known as eyases) can't leave the nest. During that time,

Young eyases depend on both parent falcons to give them enough food.

the tiercel takes his prey back to the eyrie. Later, the growing eyases will need more food. Both parents will be kept busy feeding them.

Falcons burn up huge amounts of energy. To stay alive, a peregrine must kill one large or two medium-sized birds each day. Once it has eaten, a peregrine often sits quietly in a favorite tree. Later, it may soar skyward in loops and figure eights. Bird lovers tell us the peregrine is saying, "I feel great! I want the whole world to know it!"

A bird with few natural enemies

In nature, peregrines have few enemies. Large owls have been known to hunt and kill young peregrines. Except for the largest predators, other birds usually leave the peregrine alone. Flocks of small birds sometimes gang up on a peregrine. Their aim is to drive the predator out of their territory. The peregrine usually leaves—but it may return later.

Most peregrines die from accident or disease. A bad landing means a broken wing or some lost feathers. Without good wings and flight feathers, the falcon cannot fly well enough to hunt. Lice are another danger. The peregrines control the pests by taking a daily bath. Then they preen by running each feather through their beaks. This removes dirt and lice. Peregrines also catch illnesses caused by parasites. The parasites come from their favorite food birds such as pigeons and doves.

Humans are the greatest danger to peregrine falcons. Falconers rob their nests. Hunters shoot them out of the sky with shotguns. Poisons used to control insects also kill them. For a time, it looked as though the peregrine's life cycle would be ended forever.

Human activities are the greatest danger for the peregrine.

CHAPTER THREE:

Peregrine falcons have been on earth for thousands of years. During this time these swift birds have become very successful predators. Their life cycle begins anew with the first warm days of spring.

Early spring brings new life

The young tiercel returns to his rocky eyrie in early March. He is three years old, ready to mate for the first time. His first task is to mark out his territory. Flying from spot to spot, his sharp cries warn other tiercels to stay clear. But still the tiercel calls and calls.

Finally, a female flies by, drawn by the wailing cry. The tiercel puts on a show for her. He climbs, dives, and does lovely loops. To finish his courtship, he kills a robin and offers it to her. The falcon accepts the gift. The tiercel clucks to her in a soft voice. The pair will stay together until one of them dies.

Next, the tiercel shows his eyrie to his mate. The ledge is on a cliff high above the river. The female doesn't like it. She flies to another ledge and scrapes at the dirt. The male joins her and they scrape out a hollow. That's all the nest they will build. Their eggs have tough shells that don't break easily.

The spring days pass. The peregrines bathe, preen, and hunt together. Several weeks later, they mate. The female lays four small, round eggs. The eggs are a creamy-red color, marked with dark brown spots. The female fluffs up the soft feathers on her chest and covers the eggs. The eggs must be kept warm. When she leaves the nest, the tiercel takes her place. The female also turns the eggs every once in a while. That allows the unborn eyases to develop properly. Two crows land nearby, eager to eat the eggs. The tiercel swoops in to defend his eyrie. The crows fly away, scared off by the tiercel's attack.

Four weeks later, the eggs are ready to hatch. Each unborn eyas has a sharp "egg tooth" on its beak. The eyas uses the tooth to cut its way out of the hard shell. It takes a long time. When it finally breaks out, the new-born falcon is wet and has no feathers. Its head flops over on its weak neck. The other eggs hatch within a few hours. The eyases soon dry out. They look soft and fuzzy in their downy coats. The female cleans up the nest and keeps the eyases warm.

The eyases are born with a big appetite. The falcon feeds them strips of meat. The young ones swallow the meat in one gulp. The eyases weigh only one ounce (28 g) at birth. A week later, they've grown to six ounces (170 g). Their first fuzz gives way to a rough

Eyases are born with a coat of down.

coat of white down. At three weeks, the first feathers appear. The eyases now push each other and screech for food. The falcon and the tiercel work overtime to catch enough game.

One eyas is smaller than its nest mates. The others sometimes grab its share of the food. During feeding time one day, the larger eyases push the smaller one off the ledge. Unable to fly, it falls to the rocks far below

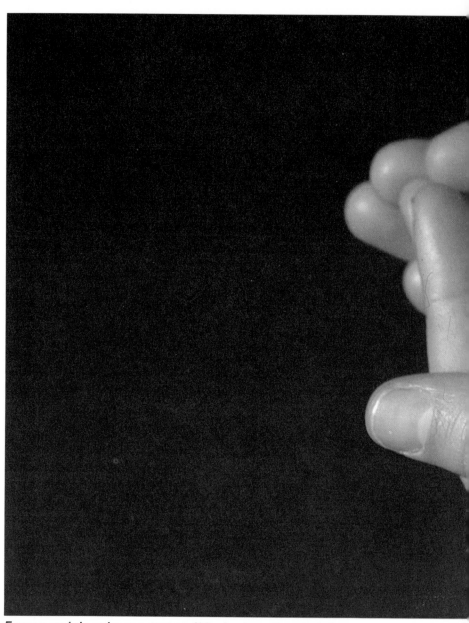

Eyases weigh only one ounce (28 g) when they hatch.

the eyrie. Meanwhile, the other eyases stretch and flap their wings. They're building up their flying muscles.

By the fifth week, the eyases have a full set of brown feathers. They're ready to fly. The falcon brings meat, but she doesn't drop it to them. She flies back and forth, just out of reach. The hungry eyases jump and scream at her. Finally, the largest female jumps off the ledge. Instinct tells her what to do. She flaps her wings and wobbles through the air. Minute by minute, she improves. The falcon drops the meat to her. The new flier grabs it as it falls. Soon all the eyases are flying.

The young peregrines must now learn to hunt. A week later, a male dives at a woodpecker. He misses. He climbs and tries again. On his fourth try, the young tiercel catches a slow-flying wood pigeon. After that, his aim improves rapidly. His sisters quickly learn the same skills.

The first summer

Summer brings longer, warmer days. The peregrine family wakes with the first light. For awhile the birds sit quietly in their eyrie. Then, one at a time, they glide down to a nearby stream. They like a spot with a sandy bottom and about six inches (15 cm) of water. They flutter in the cold water, splashing like little kids. The bath washes away lice and helps keep their feathers clean.

The peregrines return to their eyrie. They preen for

awhile and dry their feathers. After an hour's nap, they make a few lazy flights near the eyrie. Each day, they practice their hunting skills. The eyases dive at insects and falling leaves. The young tiercel catches a sparrow, but drops it. Peregrines seem to keep playtime separate from hunting time.

The family knows the limits of its territory. Their hunting grounds range twenty miles (32 km) from the eyrie in all directions. The peregrines don't hunt in another family's territory. If too many falcons hunted in the same place, the smaller birds would leave. Even now, the songbirds are learning to hide when the peregrines glide overhead.

Each peregrine family has its own hunting style. These peregrines fly a crisscross pattern until they make a kill. Other peregrines fly in long, straight lines. The eyases pick up some good tricks. Sometimes they fly past a hard-to-catch bird. The bird relaxes, thinking the danger is past. Then the peregrine turns back and picks off its careless prey. The eyases also learn to attack with the sun behind them. Blinded by the sun, the prey is easier to catch.

Summer is time for another peregrine game. The hot sun creates updrafts of warm air. The peregrines ride these columns of air to great heights. Then they glide lazily down in big circles. They also ride the wind when it blows hard. All this time, the young falcons are growing stronger. When fall comes, they must be ready for a long flight to warmer lands.

The fall migration

The peregrines awake one morning to find frost on the ground. Soon the birds they feed on will fly south for the winter. Cold weather doesn't bother the peregrines. But they cannot stay where there is little food to catch. One by one, the older birds leave. The young peregrines are now on their own. Finally, they also head south. Instinct tells them when to leave and where to go. Some fly with other peregrines. Others join flocks of smaller birds.

The peregrine family flies south to Florida. Some of their tundra cousins will go all the way to South America. The older birds return to the same territories they lived in last year. The younger birds find their own winter habitat. On the west coast, Peale's peregrines often winter in their own eyries. They find enough small birds and rodents for food to get through the winter. Peregrines that live in cities may also stay close to home. Fat, slow-flying pigeons keep these city falcons well fed.

For the migrating peregrines, winter is like a second summer. The birds hunt, feed, play, and preen. Finally, spring begins to melt the northern snows. Somehow, the peregrines know that it's time to fly north again. Left to themselves, the peregrines might have gone on this way forever.

Peregrines that live in the North during the summer, spend the winter in the South.

CHAPTER FOUR:

A tall, bearded naturalist hid at the top of the cliff. On a ledge below him, a peregrine was feeding two hungry eyases. The naturalist made notes as he watched. He was part of a plan to save these beautiful falcons. He needed to know everything there was to know about them.

Naturalists hope to help peregrines by closely studying them.

The eyases ate their fill and quieted down. The adult birds were off hunting. They no longer worried about the man who watched them day after day. The naturalist had a moment to rest. His eyes closed, but his mind was still on peregrines.

An old, much-loved sport

The naturalist knew that humans have liked peregrines since early times. People in China and Persia trained falcons for hunting over four thousand years ago. Falconry spread to Egypt, to North Africa, and around the world. In the Middle Ages, flying falcons was a much-loved sport. Falconers also trained other birds, but the peregrine was their favorite. Old paintings show nobles riding out from a castle for a day's sport. Each knight carries a hooded falcon on his arm. The ladies weren't left out. They carried small falcons known as merlins.

Falconry began to die out after the 1600's. Fields were fenced in. Guns made hunting with birds seem like a waste of time. The skills of the falconer weren't lost, however. Today, desert nomads in Africa and Asia still train falcons for the hunt. These people use falcons

Falcons have been trained to hunt for over four thousand years.

33

to hunt deer as well as birds. The peregrine cannot kill a deer, but it dives at the deer's head again and again. The deer is confused by this attack. It becomes easy game for the hunter's dogs.

Training a falcon

Today, peregrine falcons are an endangered species. Federal laws punish anyone who traps or harms them. Some states do allow falconers to keep other birds of prey, such as prairie falcons and kestrels. A falconer must first have a bird to train, however. Years ago, falconers often took young birds from the nest. Raised by humans, these falcons sometimes became too tame to be good hunters. Many falconers prefer to start with passage falcons (young birds making their first migration). In ancient times, passage falcons were caught by putting raw meat under a basket. When the bird flew in to grab the meat, the falconer sprang the trap. Modern hunters use nets to trap the birds.

Training a falcon takes time, love, and hard work. The naturalist thought about his first passage peregrine. That was back before peregrines were an endangered species. He spent the first weeks taming his tiercel. The bird had a natural fear of humans which had to be overcome. Next, the naturalist taught the falcon to perch on his gloved hand. He fed the bird when it jumped

Falconry takes time and patience.

to his arm. The falcon also learned to accept the leather hood over its head. The hood kept the bird quiet when the naturalist was carrying it.

Next, the naturalist taught the peregrine to hunt. He tied pieces of meat to the end of a long rope. Then he swung the rope in a circle. The tiercel soon learned to dive at this lure. The naturalist fed the bird each time it caught the lure. The tiercel seemed to enjoy the game. It learned that food came from the man, not the lure.

Peregrines usually learn to trust their handlers within a few weeks.

Finally, the naturalist trained the tiercel for free flight. The falcon could have flown away, but it didn't. It flew upward, then dived at the swinging lure. Later, it learned to hunt live birds. When it caught a fat pigeon, the tiercel brought it back to its trainer. The bird liked the fresh red meat the man gave it better than the feathery pigeon!

The peregrines and DDT

Disaster struck the peregrine falcon in the 1950's. A 1942 count reported 275 active peregrine eyries east of the Rocky Mountains. Experts believed that about two hundred eyases should survive each year. But a new count in 1964, could not find a single live American peregrine eyas!

A study of the eyries showed that the females were laying eggs. But the eggs didn't hatch. The shells were too thin. Some of them broke when the falcon sat on them. Others didn't have enough food in the yolk. The eyases died before they grew to full size. With no young birds being born, the species seemed doomed.

Scientists knew the cause of the disaster. Pelicans and other birds that ate fish were already dying. The problem started when farmers killed insects with DDT. Rain washed the leftover poison into the rivers, lakes, and oceans. There, tiny plants and animals absorbed it. Fish ate the plants, and birds ate the fish. Each animal stored up DDT in its body. In birds, the poison kept the female's body from using calcium. And calcium was needed to make eggshells.

At first, the naturalists didn't see how DDT could affect peregrines. After all, peregrines eat other birds, not fish. Their studies soon turned up the answer. The peregrines got their DDT from birds that ate poisoned fish and insects. The government outlawed DDT for most uses in the U.S. But no one held out much hope for the peregrines. DDT stays in the soil for a long time. The peregrine would be gone before the poison was gone.

Project peregrine

Peregrine lovers weren't ready to give up. Heinz Meng decided to raise peregrines in cages. Most naturalists told him he was crazy! They said that peregrines would only mate in their natural habitat. But Meng knew that a German falconer had bred peregrines in the 1940's. Meng started in 1964, but he had many failures. Finally, in 1971, his peregrines hatched a tiny eyas. Meng was overjoyed. Peregrines could be bred in captivity!

At Cornell University in New York, Dr. Tom Cade started Project Peregrine. Cornell raised money to build a long barn for his peregrines. The barn had two-story "apartments" that made good eyries. Meng and other falconers donated birds of mating age. Cade also wanted to raise his own mating pairs. The government let him take a few Peale's peregrines from Alaska. A female named Cadey was one of the eyases he found there.

In 1973, Cadey mated with a tiercel named Heyoka. She laid four eggs. Cade took the eggs away. Cadey laid four more. Again, the naturalist removed the eggs. Cadey fussed at him, but she laid four more eggs! Cade and his helpers put the eggs in an incubator. Three weeks later, Project Peregrine's first eyases pecked through their shells.

These people are raising peregrines in Jackson Hole, Wyoming.

This peregrine is being banded as part of a study in Alaska.

For two weeks, the team members fed and cared for the eyases. Then they put the little ones back with Cadey and Heyoka. The adult birds took good care of the eyases. That year, twenty eyases lived and learned to fly in the barn. But would the young peregrines learn to hunt on their own?

One of the young tiercels answered that question. Taken outdoors to fly, he began to dive at pigeons. Instinct told him that small birds were his natural prey. A few weeks later, the tiercel flew up to chase away another predator from his territory. This time, he didn't come back.

In 1978, the project produced ninety-five eyases. Cade and his helpers began releasing the peregrines. They fed them for awhile, but the falcons soon learned to hunt on their own. The Project birds began nesting on some nearby cliffs. Peregrines were once more living wild in the eastern United States.

Peregrines move to the city

The naturalist lying on the cliff was part of another project. The plan was to put peregrines into a new habitat: America's big cities. The record showed that peregrines had done well in Montreal, New York, and

The peregrine falcon is slowly coming back from the edge of extinction.

other cities. In 1981, a team turned nine peregrines loose in Los Angeles, California. Eight of the birds survived the first year.

The peregrines found their own eyries. Several falcons nested on the ledges of the Plaza Building in Westwood. Two more picked out the Union Bank skyscraper in downtown Los Angeles. Another bird moved out to the coast at Marina del Rey. Local citizens couldn't believe their eyes. They looked up to see peregrines chasing pigeons down busy Wilshire Boulevard!

The project members are still watching these falcons. The young birds have laid eggs, but none have hatched. It's good news when a peregrine lays eggs. At the present time, these rare eggs are worth up to $2,000.00 each! In 1985, the naturalists tried a test with two eyases hatched in an incubator. They put the young birds in one of the eyries. The peregrines adopted the eyases and raised them. If all goes well, the birds will soon be hatching their own eggs.

Naturalists still have their fingers crossed. Thus far, the news is good. The peregrine falcon is coming back from the edge of extinction.

MAP:

The shaded areas show where
most peregrine falcons live.

INDEX/GLOSSARY:

DDT 9, 10, 14, 16, 37, 38 — *A powerful poison for killing insects. DDT is now outlawed for most uses. Once it enters the soil and water, DDT also poisons fish, birds, and mammals.*

ENDANGERED SPECIES 34 — *An animal that is in danger of becoming extinct.*

EYAS 18, 19, 22, 23, 24, 26, 27, 30, 31, 37, 38, 39, 41, 44 — *A young male or female falcon.*

EYRIE 13, 16, 19, 21, 22, 23, 26, 27, 28, 37, 39, 44 — *The nesting place of any predatory bird.*

EXTINCTION 7, 9, 42, 44 — *The loss of a species, as when the last animal of that species dies.*

FALCON 10, 21, 23, 26, 37 — *A female peregrine falcon.*

FALCONRY 9, 31, 35 — *The sport of hunting with falcons.*

HABITAT 14, 15, 28, 38, 41 — *The place where an animal makes its home.*

INCUBATOR 39, 44 — *A box in which a bird's eggs can be kept warm so that they will hatch properly.*

INSTINCT 41 — *Behaviors an animal knows from the time it's born.*

MIGRATION 15, 28 — *The yearly movement of animals from one habitat to another.*

MOLTING 11 — *When a bird loses its feathers so that new feathers can grow to replace them.*

NATURALIST 5, 9, 13, 16, 17, 30, 31, 34, 36, 37, 38, 39, 41, 44 — *A scientist who studies plants and animals.*

PARASITES 19 — *Any insects, germs, or worms that feed on a bird or other animal.*

PASSAGE FALCONS 34 — *Wild falcons trapped during their first migration south.*

PREDATOR 8, 16, 17, 19, 21, 41 — *An animal that lives by preying on other animals.*

PREENING 19, 22, 26, 28 — *When a falcon cleans and smooths its feathers with its beak.*

INDEX/GLOSSARY:

WILDLIFE
HABITS & HABITAT

READ AND ENJOY THE SERIES:

If you would like to know more about all kinds of wildlife, you should take a look at the other books in this series.

You'll find books on bald eagles and other birds. Books on alligators and other reptiles. There are books about deer and other big-game animals. And there are books about sharks and other creatures that live in the ocean.

In all of the books you will learn that life in the wild is not easy. But you will also learn what people can do to help wildlife survive. So read on!